FEARLESS
THE STORY OF
Daphne Caruana Galizia

Written and Illustrated by Gattaldo

Otter-Barry BOOKS

In a house by the sea, on the island of Malta,
lived a little girl named Daphne,
together with her mum, dad and three sisters.

At bedtime Daphne would ask her father to tell the story
of her great-great-great-great-grandfather, Captain Salvatore Vella.

CAPTAIN SALVATORE VELLA

The Captain and his brother had stood up
to the Emperor Napoleon's garrison in 1798 to save their country.

Every year, in the weeks before their village feast,
Daphne and her sisters liked nothing more
than to spend hours cutting up magazines
into confetti to throw from their balcony.

Daphne loved these colourful magazines
and the stories they told.

One day, she told herself,
she too would use pictures and words
to tell important stories.

Daphne grew to love reading
and getting lost in imaginative stories.

Wherever she was, you'd always find her
with her nose in a book.

Books taught Daphne
never to let people think for her.

She loved the freedom of asking questions
and then making up her own mind.

Daphne and her friends
saw bad things happening
in their country.

They believed that they
could change people's lives
for the better by
peaceful protest.

One day, at a protest gathering, Daphne was arrested and put in a dark cell for two nights.

She was frightened but she was determined never to give up.

At the age of twenty-one,
Daphne married Peter,
a young lawyer and fellow protester.
They had three children,
Matthew, Andrew and Paul.

Daphne and Peter taught their children
to have enquiring minds
and always to fight injustice.

Daphne started writing
for a national newspaper.

There were very few
women journalists
at that time.

But Daphne worked hard
and proved she was
one of the best.

Daphne was not afraid to uncover wrongdoing.
That is what a good journalist does.

PROTECT OUR COUNTRYSIDE

JOBS ON MERIT

She did not flinch,
even when her enemy was powerful and mighty.

Many people who agreed with Daphne
were too frightened to say so.

She often felt alone in her struggle.
But she was confident
she had truth on her side.

Daphne's enemies did everything in their power
to prevent her from exposing their misdeeds.

They **hassled** her in the streets, they called her a **witch**,
they **burnt** her front door, they **killed** her pet dog, Messalina.

Daphne wasn't going to let these people
stop her telling the truth.

The more they tried,
the stronger she felt.

Daphne's writing
travelled the world
and inspired more and more
people to speak out.

Daphne had persuaded others
to continue her work...

and make our world a better place.

From left:
1. Daphne (right) with her mother and sisters
2. Peter took this photo of Daphne and children, Andrew, Paul and Matthew while on holiday
3. Portrait of Daphne
4. Sisters – Mandy, Helene, Daphne and Corinne

Photographs courtesy of
The Caruana Galizia Foundation
except for portrait photo © Pippa Zammit Cutajar

Daphne Caruana Galizia 1964 - 2017

Daphne's story is important for us all. At a time when even governments put out 'fake news', she stands out as someone who refused to be silenced, uncovering organised crime, money laundering and political corruption.

Born in Malta's seaside town of Sliema, Daphne became interested in her country's political goings-on at a young age, joining others in peaceful protests. During one such demonstration when Daphne was just 19, she was arrested and held in custody for 36 hours on made-up charges including assaulting the police. The magistrate found her innocent and dismissed all the charges.

In 1985, Daphne married Peter, a lawyer and fellow protester. They had three sons – Matthew, Andrew and Paul. Wanting to do more with her time, Daphne pitched a few articles to a national newspaper and the editor took her on as a regular Sunday columnist.

In one of her early articles, Daphne wrote, *"Fear, unfortunately, is the greatest enemy of freedom of expression – and of dialogue"*. She never let fear get in the way. Daphne signed her newspaper column at a time when others preferred to stay silent or remain anonymous.

In 2008, Daphne started her own blog to publish

Author's message

Hello. I wrote this book because I wanted to share with you the story of my friend Daphne. Many years ago when I was still a young man, I read Daphne's newspaper column regularly. I decided to write her a letter to say how much I admired her writing. To my surprise she wrote back and we became penfriends.

Although by this time we lived in different countries, we took turns to visit and kept our friendship alive. We talked about a lot of things. We did not always agree on everything, but we were always open to each other's opinion. It's always important to listen and understand before making up your mind.

I miss Daphne very much but she is in my heart and thoughts.

xxx *Gattaldo*

stories of wrongdoing that her editors were scared to print. Those whose misdeeds were uncovered threatened Daphne, killed three of her dogs, attempted to burn her family home twice, and had her bank account frozen.

But Daphne never gave up. Finally, on 16th October, 2017, she was killed by a bomb placed under her car. Whoever ordered this shocking crime may have thought that no more would be heard of Daphne. Instead, her brave and brilliant example has become a worldwide inspiration to everyone who believes that truth should win out over lies, and that nobody is above the law.

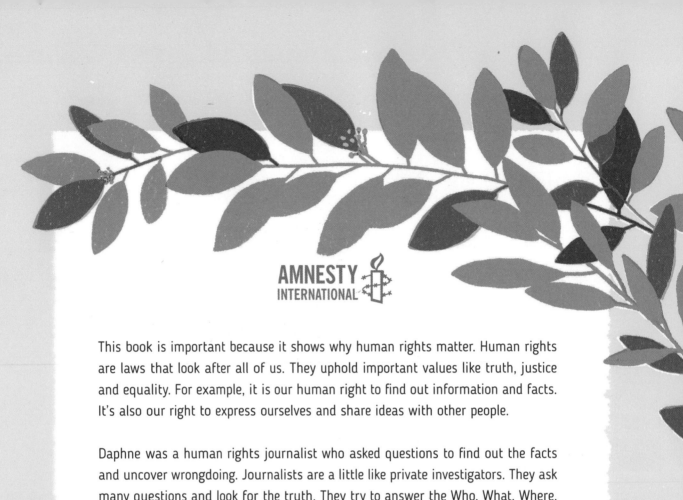

AMNESTY INTERNATIONAL

This book is important because it shows why human rights matter. Human rights are laws that look after all of us. They uphold important values like truth, justice and equality. For example, it is our human right to find out information and facts. It's also our right to express ourselves and share ideas with other people.

Daphne was a human rights journalist who asked questions to find out the facts and uncover wrongdoing. Journalists are a little like private investigators. They ask many questions and look for the truth. They try to answer the Who, What, Where, When and Why. They help us all to understand what really happened so that we can stand up for justice.

We can all use our right to ask questions, find out the truth and say what we think. Let's make the world a better place. Amnesty International is a movement of millions of ordinary people around the world standing up for human rights. Find out more and access lots of free and fun education resources at

www.amnesty.org.uk/education